MW00928027

GROWING

GOLD

By Syrah Kai

Growing Gold

© 2019 Syrah Kai. All rights reserved.

Read more at:

Instagram: @Syrah.Kai

www.syrahkai.com

Cover designed by the lovely

Monika Brenner

www.monikabrenner.com

Growing Gold

Growing Gold

Dedicated to my rock in shining armour.
You saw something in me I thought was only
an illusion.

My formula for greatness in a human being is amor fati: that one wants nothing to be different, not forward, not backward, not in all eternity.

Friedrich Nietzsche

Contents

Note From The Author

How many times have you hit rock bottom, either from loss, heartbreak or some form of failure? We have all been there for several reasons. I want you to know, you're never stuck at the bottom of the barrel, no matter how deep. You have the skills you need to find your way out. They are hidden inside you but discovering them is a journey that isn't always pleasant. Hitting rock bottom, or feeling close to it, is not in and of itself a bad thing. I believe it is an extremely powerful moment, a catalyst for massive life change. And it's up to you to make the most of it, and if you do, you'll unlock an unimaginable inner power and the ability to turn your purple bruises into glowing golden wings.

This book is a compilation of poems that highlights the steps and stages for spiritual recovery and personal transformation. This all comes from a journey I have been on, since I was a child, until now, nearing my 30s. My experiences always feed me spiritually and creatively. Not only do my direct trauma and sickness affect me, the experiences of those around me, those who have confided in me over the years have left imprints on me emotionally. I empathize deeply, carried their hurt inside me. But the time has come for me to let it all out. Let it go and learn to breathe.

The struggle is real, but you must know, that even the most supported individual must still fight their demons on their own. Please read these poems with an open heart. Whatever emotions, if any, flood you—feel them. You need to feel to heal. This book isn't only for those who are at their lowest lows. Anyone who is human, who has felt any degree of hardship can connect to these poems. So as long as you're not a filthy rich robot, there is something in this book for you, too.

If this collection of poetry moves you to any degree, I compel you to share it with someone you think will also appreciate them. I have taken these private and personal poems and shared them to the world not to have them fall on deaf ears. So, spread the word, post it on social media, leave an honest review, or recommend it to a friend. The ripple effect is magical, and once inspired it never ends.

This book is divided into 4 chapters, each one explores a different state of rebirth. Chapter 1, The Eclipse, touches on the fall into the abyss, when the light is blocked and diminished. Hope is lost as you lose your balance and stumble down a frightening new path. It is pure chaos This can take the form of many triggers, most often loss, failure or an emotional wound. It's a downward spiral that seems to lead to nowhere, but it doesn't last forever, there is a bottom and eventually you'll reach it.

Chapter 2, The Longest Shadow, dives into the purgatory of pain. The time after you've hit rock bottom and have been left rather disoriented, confused, not sure who to turn to. At this stage of metaphorical death you wander around the shadows. Most often this is when depression really sets in, at least it was for me.

Chapter 3, Creatures Of The Dark, introduces you to your demons as you might meet them in this process of injury and healing. This may manifest as an ego death, facing your fears, or meeting others who embody what you need to change, people who are hurting like you. People who act as mirrors. Here is when you have the chance to face the music and be honest with yourself. Instead of ignoring the pain, hoping it'll just go away, you can address it, clean it, even if it stings. If you can do this, meet your trauma face to face, forgive yourself, and let go of your pain, you are on your way to restoring light and climbing out of this dreary place.

Chapter 4, Becoming Light, talks about just that, becoming light. Once you've taken responsibility for your mistakes, forgiven yourself as well as others, and have processed the pain, you are ripe for growth. It's not easy to get to this point, sometimes we are stuck in the shadows for quite a long time, each of us has a different journey. But if you can muster the strength, the hope, and confidence to climb out of the hole, you will see how all this torment can be used and turned into gold. From your pain comes power, from your scars comes gold. You can resurrect and redeem yourself, stronger and wiser. This is the cycle of our lives, and it will continue forever. But you have the power of awareness. If you can experience pain consciously and work through the process, you will be reborn glistening. I hope somewhere in this book are the words you need to trigger the fertilization of potential. I hope you see the gold in you and all you've been through

Chapter 1 The Eclipse

Growing Gold

Some stories

are meant to be shared,

some

      should stay hidden—

mine begs to be told

but remain cryptic

      within reason.

Some stories

Growing Gold

Chaos is a lady
with an embellished sword,

she doesn't believe
in gun fights

she'd rather stab you
in the heart

and watch as
        your last breath
                leaves this world

Lady chaos

Growing Gold

I apologize now
　　　　for this starts as a sad story
　　　　with no reason behind it
because life has no warnings,

Together we will fall
　　　　in love and terror
　　　　land on hard ground
on broken bits of mirrors,
but if you can grind through the pain
　　　　and stand up again
　　　　we have a fighting chance
of making it to the end,

Where rumours say
　　　　the light will break
　　　　blindness will be lifted
and demons will be slain

Until the end

Growing Gold

And so,
      we fall,
into the depths of chaos
      a realm with no respect
      for the rules of order
up is inside
           and down is out
      I wish you farewell—
because once you fall
      into what some think is hell
        all that will survive
are the parts of you
      that you've never seen
           in yourself

Hell

Growing Gold

Be careful what you wish for
because nothing is free
       that love you've been dreaming of
       the success you've been yearning
       the peace you've been begging to be
       the inspiration you're searching for
it all comes at a price
and the cost is a transitory state
of confusion and misery
so hold tight,
       empty your pockets
         and soul
you've made some tall orders
and with it comes
       a taller toll

Transformation fee

Growing Gold

Chaos is more
            than pure confusion
            and lack of coordination

It's true potential
            volatile
            and explosive

It's life before birth
            the seed
            that fosters order

Chaos is hell only to those
            who can't let go
            of the constant need
for control

Pure chaos

Growing Gold

There is a trigger

within us

an uncomfortable fire

    that switches from a flicker

        to explosive desire

And while you try to avoid

      setting off the alarms

        the sooner you face

        your demons

the sooner you can pass

          the guards

Triggers

Growing Gold

You did your best
just to survive
but that's not what life

              was meant for

so now you are here,

losing again

because you've forgotten how

              to genuinely give in

Survival

Growing Gold

When the foundation has cracks

but you still keep building

don't cry at the collapse

because it was you who was

refurnishing on the inside

and adding new stories

when the basement was leaking

and the walls were peeling

on the floors you refused to visit

Weak aesthetics

Growing Gold

If you never learn

           to fall down

you never learn to get back

      up

and many of us

were loved too much

by parents who

      held us so often

we never had to learn

      to walk

Loved too much

Growing Gold

Maybe the reason you are
falling
      apart
is because you didn't wake up
and wish yourself
a good morning
      with a cup of healing
and a toast to another day
      of breathing in life
      and breathing out blessings
so now you are dark
and unfeeling
      and all I can tell you is
you better kiss yourself goodnight
and hope to have sweet dreams
because you'll wake again
and nothing will change
until you wish yourself a good morning
      with a hot cup of healing

A hot cup

Growing Gold

When you try to carry the world
                  and all its woes
upon your puny human shoulders
                   you're bound to
collapse
for you are not Atlas
       it is not your curse
            to carry all of that
and if you don't shrug it off
eventually your spirit will be crushed
until you figure out for yourself
       that you only have two hands
and that's more than *enough*

Carry what you can

28

Growing Gold

None of it happened

it was all in my head

but then again

        all of it is

Trauma

Growing Gold

Looking for socks
at the bottom of a drawer
has me throwing underwear
      in every direction
wishing I had paired them before
I curse my habit of taking the easy road
and even though I always find
my missing counterpart
      I still end up
with a bigger mess on the floor
and all could have been avoided
if I had paid attention
      to order more

Bitter retrospect

Growing Gold

Everything I thought
        was safe and real
turned out to be
           another trap
disguised as an opportunity
            to heal

Trapped

Growing Gold

I hate puzzles

because they demand

     to be completed

when I can't even find all of

     my own

missing pieces

Puzzle pieces

Growing Gold

Have you lost your mind
        or just your heart?
I'd give you a piece of mine
        but I'm also falling apart
have you looked inside
at your darkest parts
where you put bad memories
        and failed attempts at art?
Sometimes we find
the secret to peace
deep inside the storm
        in the eye
            of insanity

The eye of the storm

33

Growing Gold

I followed the moon
all the way home
until she
            could no longer
keep up with me

Mooning

Growing Gold

The nature of black

is to devour

      all that is white

to absorb its profundity

and spits it out

      into an effortless night

Night light

Growing Gold

Darkness is nothing
but nothing is all
we have
      for certain
and if I'm certain
about one thing
it's that
      nothing lies
behind the curtain

Certain about nothing

Growing Gold

Can't you see
        how the night
        and the morning
always seem
to accidentally meet
mixing their elements
like oil and paint
        tearing open holes in
        your dark blue sheets
when was the last time
you made an effort to greet
the sun and the moon
        with a cup of tea?

Sun tea

Growing Gold

Like a bad acid trip
all the good was sucked
                out of my life
light bulbs I had just changed
                suddenly died
windows I kept open were
                jammed shut,
                        tight
and with a rapid swirl
all that I cherished
was suddenly denied
who pulled the plug
                on my light
and how can I fix it
now that I'm blind?

Blindsight

Growing Gold

As a child I was drawn
     to small

     dark

     spaces

I'd crawl under coffee tables

and sit in linen closets

there was comfort in the shadows

where my eyes couldn't know

     if they were open

     or closed

that's when my imagination

would roar the loudest

but now I'm big

and those spaces are still small

and if I crawl under a table now

people will start to think

     something is wrong

Outgrowing the little things

Growing Gold

I was a small girl
around seven years old
laying in the grass
breathing in August air
       I was pondering upon the clouds
       watching sunlight tickle the trees
       when the darkest of truths
       revealed itself to me

This moment is fleeting
my childhood is counting down
       one day I will be working
          and summers will just be
       another season to sweat it out
and this fraction of a second
       is all that counts

Shaken by this truth
and slightly angry
       that it came at all
I jumped up from

Growing Gold

my bed of grass

and rejoined my friends

in the park

I wanted to scream for them

    to never stop playing

warn them that our joy was secretly

    waning

But as I sprinted back to the sandbox

    I decided to hold my tongue

    and instead preserve the present

    for everyone

they suggested a new game to play

and asked me to be "it"

so I chased my friends as I tried my best

to make this moment last

as long as I lived

Last days

Growing Gold

The night eats light

like cereal for breakfast

bowl after bowl

until the ocean is bloated

       and rises to the surface

the sky swells up

until it cracks open

and little specks of light

       sweat out emotion

like salty tears

they sometimes fall from heaven

when the night eats the light

     like it's cereal for breakfast

A light breakfast

Growing Gold

My biggest downfall

is not being able to

                    fall down

without taking someone

                    down with me

Downfall

Growing Gold

I failed

because I tried

so I promised myself

      I'd never try again

and instead

of asking why

I vowed to figure out

      when

so the next time

      I strike

I'm sure to break skin

Failure and revenge

Growing Gold

So you couldn't live up

to your expectations

      and even worse

you disappointed your parents

I'm not going to scold you

and give lectures on the value

      of diligence

I only want to say

      congratulations

I wish you the best

on your journey

      to realization

now that you've let the world down

you can finally dive in

to your true

    imagination

When all is lost, imagine

Growing Gold

I found myself
on the fullest moon
with a sudden smack
          of clarity
the light I had been
          holding back
decided to resurface
with vengeance—
          a new kind of luminosity
a humble glow
patiently reflecting

The light before death

Growing Gold

I laid awake
under the chandelier
of a starry night
with hot streams of
    moonlight
        falling from my eyes
I cried to the heavens
and she cried for me
having watched me sacrifice
so much of my life
supporting everyone else
forgetting
    I, too,
      am alive

Starry eyes

Growing Gold

I was selling my soul

for a sense of security

       that did not belong to me

but was on loan

from someone who

never missed an opportunity

to remind me of their

       incessant generosity

Generous debt

Growing Gold

If you never die

        how can you live

if forever was everlasting

        you'd have no reason to give

so release your fear

        of reaching the end

because the end is the beginning

        over and over again

Once upon an ending

Growing Gold

Rest in peace
the darkest pieces
of who I used to be
      may you see the light
      and meet your mastery
for now,
my body
will be buried
by all my bad memories
      my flesh will decompose
      and turn into something gross
but I have hope
that in time this grave
will be the home
of something new
      that will grow

Rest in peace, the old me

Growing Gold

Growing Gold

Growing Gold

Chapter 2 The Longest Shadow

Growing Gold

The funny thing about darkness
is how it plays
    tricks on
        our eyes
and that innocent rustling bush
suddenly becomes
    a bear
and you run for your life
chased by nothing
but your fears
    and lies

Afraid of the dark

Growing Gold

The night is but
one long shadow
    we share

One bloated spider
with legs covered
    in spikes of hair

The night is but
one long
      mystery novel
keeping you on edge

Mystery

Growing Gold

The shade of the night
shields the light
    from my eyes
how safe I finally feel
now that I can
    hide behind my lies

Night lies

Growing Gold

Have you ever woken up
before sunrise
and felt confused
          with no sense of time?
well that's what it feels like
when you slowly lose your mind,
          clocks speak in tongues
and the public is a catastrophe
all that makes sense
is the dungeon you've built
      in your dark and damp
          heart cavity

Dark heart

Growing Gold

Your longest shadow comes
just before light decides to break
     and either illuminates the sky
     or sinks into the horizon's grave
your longest shadow is a
telling sign that stars are falling
     and slowing time
as your heart eclipses the
last hour
of light
     there will be new creatures
     to meet as you enter
     the endless night
your longest shadow seems
     heavy for now
          but wait until the darkness settles
          and you have to face yourself
you'll miss your phantom companion
     once the demons come out
          you can't hide from those
          who live in the dark

Growing Gold

their eyes are well adjusted
and will see you all curled up
like a lost child in a park
you have to face your fears
until the light survives the dark

     and your longest shadow comes back
     like a dear old friend
and together you will implode
becoming all kinds of fire
          at once
     burning down barriers,
     saluting the sun
breathe in the mist
and let the night go
     you and your longest shadow
          can finally feel the gold.

Your longest shadow

Growing Gold

The night can make you do
unforgettable things
survival comes
        with zero shame,
        and whispers can mean
        anything

Night train

Growing Gold

There's a pit in my stomach
but not the nervous kind
it's one that I've been digging
while I play with the idea
     of jumping inside
let the world turn without me
let the seasons pass by
leave me here and forget me
     I need some time to die

I need some time

Growing Gold

The diamond gets all the glory
but what about the pressure?
    that gem couldn't shine
without my crushing intention
    I am force,
I am how the diamond is formed

        without my efforts
      you'd still be glass and dust
    nothing but an exhale
        upon the earth
        who am I?
      I am the furnace
      where your heart is born

Diamond dust

Growing Gold

 I feel consumed by a sense
of defeated loneliness
despite being in a crowd

        I feel so alone

With my heart sinking
like a stone you've thrown
    all you can do is watch
as I start to lose touch
    with everything real
and the ability feel

Skipping stones

Growing Gold

I started to drown

                as soon as I asked for help

I opened my mouth

not knowing I'd let

                my last breath out

and now my lungs are soaked

and my voice has nowhere to go

        so I scream inside

        as I fall behind

the surface tension

of oxygen and ocean

Drowning out

Growing Gold

What brings you to this land
        of sorrow
who packed your bags,
do you have anything to declare,
like a carton of memoires,
        or your childhood bear?

Please submit yourself
for selective searching
we suspect you are hiding something
    that needs unearthing

Crossing the border

Growing Gold

I'm about to hit the bottom
of a dark and cold placé
I hear the echo of voices
and remember
        loving them once
but now they are murmurs
distorted above the surface
        and I am a rock
sinking fast
leaving nothing behind
but pitiful ripples
        that eventually go deaf

Sinking fast

67

Growing Gold

Trauma is like making
French onion soup
                 after you chop
                 that many onions
                 peeling one or two
                 just doesn't hurt you
                 the same way it used to
the onions may not get to you
but god knows now
you can't stomach soup

Post traumatic soup

Growing Gold

You thought you hit rock bottom

but it was actually

    a trap door

surprise,

        surprise,

now you're going to fall

down a few more floors

Trap door

Growing Gold

 Have you destroyed everything yet?
if not,

      talk to me when you do
I am not interested in helping anyone
unless they have nothing

      left to lose

Self-destruct

Growing Gold

At the bottom of the bucket

sitting with the crabs

I told myself

    chaos is poetry

because at first glance

it doesn't make sense

but when you read between the lines

and listen to the whispers

you start to understand

    that madness

    is not crazy

and making a mess

    isn't always bad

sometimes we need to lose

    our sensibility

so we can learn to feel again

Learning from the crabs

Growing Gold

I don't want this body
    to be how I'm known
this biological contraption
    feels nothing like home
why was I given
        this flesh sentence
what crimes came with this punishment
    this figure so soft
    and slow

Body low

Growing Gold

What if I died

       in the middle of the night

and a stranger woke up in my body

how would I know

that these thoughts

      are my own

      and not the seeds

      of my imposters

am I the hard copy?

What if I'm not me?

Growing Gold

I was afraid to look in the mirror

because my reflection

      was so angry

she didn't even

recognize me

in my bloated state

of sugar-coated

      apathy

Bloated

Growing Gold

Don't hate the version of yourself
that threw you down a flight
    of endless stairs
toddlers have tantrums for a reason
        sometimes they need sleep
        sometimes they need attention
so give your lesser self
exactly what it needs
whether it's a moment of rest
or a lecture on how to handle
sharing
    this reality

Whatever you need

Growing Gold

I've never seen
someone lose face
with as much grace
     as you
does it feel good
to beg for sympathy
     down there
on your bruised knees?
I bet the attention
     secretly
makes you giddy

You enjoy my sympathy

Growing Gold

We found ourselves

on a train with no breaks

running out of track

      still refusing to say grace

      still too stubborn

to accept our fate

so we tell ourselves

     this is fine

and get comfortable

on this

      fatal freight

Afraid train

Growing Gold

 I can taste dust
in the basement of my brain
        old stale debris
raining on my face

How long has it been
since the last time I cleaned
the gutters that run
between
        my subconscious
and waking

The closet between my dreams
is overflowing with old clothes
        that no longer fit me
past journals of fear
and old projects that remain
        incomplete

Clutter

Growing Gold

This isn't just sadness

this is complete despair

this is why I can't get out of bed

or find the energy

       to wash my hair

I don't recognize my reflection

it just mocks me anyway

makes faces when I'm not looking

       calls me hurtful names

this isn't just pain

this is agony

this is why I can't go to work

       or care about money

I don't want responsibility

there's too much of it

and not enough of me

I'm better off taking shelter in my room

       my misery doesn't want company

Such misery

Growing Gold

I woke up
and wrote a song

but forgot

       I couldn't sing

so I ripped the pages

from my notebook

       and threw them to the birds

they can have the rights

and everything

I can't sing

Growing Gold

Once upon a nightmare
I fell down
    a deep
        dark
            hole
but the true horror I found
was that I've been here
            before

Once upon a nightmare

Growing Gold

 How suddenly
everything changed
one minute
there was ice cream

     melting

     dripping

staining my shoes
and the next thing I knew

     I was on fire

and all hell broke loose

All hell

Growing Gold

She did her best
to swallow her cries
but still couldn't hide
the tears that were
over throwing power
in her opalescent eyes
she could feel her heart
being torn open
and filled up with something
hot,
    sticky,
        and foreign

Heart invasion

Growing Gold

I'm peeling myself alive
exposing my raw
      untouched hide
it's too ugly to look at
please divert your eyes
this is my process of evolution
      a revolt of illusion
in secret I will shed
limbs that are rotting
             dead
as I churn in anguish
I can smell
all that must
      be left behind

Peeling

Growing Gold

Spin yourself into webs

              that block off every entrance

there is a nausea that lurks

              and demands to be heard

a rotten piece of food

              a memory or two

something is sick and burns inside you

stay still

stay low

and allow the purge to flow

the torment of transformation

              is worth its weight in gold.

Nausea webs

Growing Gold

Tears threaten to cross the border
the threshold of my fears
as I let go of my old
and tired
      ego
I open myself up
to a world of new danger

Tearing open

Growing Gold

The absurd fatigue
                of the 11th hour
the darkest night
                before dawning
exhausted from a place
                that has served its purpose
I'm ready to be still
rest,
reflect,
sleep,
and bury the carcass
                of the old me
how I loved you so deeply

Absurd fatigue

Growing Gold

When the night hits peak depth
      and darkness is darker
                than death
I'll step out into the whispers
      of the wind and clouds
because despite the eerie stillness
      the world still turns
despite my pleads and protests
      the world still turns

Still but turning

Growing Gold

The great eclipse
leaves a shadow that trembles
           bruising my lips
where night waits for no time
and seconds sit still
           like a meditating mind
I can see nothing
and feel nothing
           but smell burning
I left the stove on
and my heart cooking

Dark times

Growing Gold

Where does it go
the star that hangs low
        falling
                followed by applause
with a beautiful burst
cousins of lightning
she shimmers
and suddenly
                is gone

Fallen star

Growing Gold

Are my eyes closed

or does darkness not cease to grow

with each blink I see

specks of light

      flickering

      and forgotten

I can feel my insides turn into night

      dissolve into dusk

letting go of what used to be love

Black eyes closing

Growing Gold

There's a swollen black hole
consuming crumbs of hope
        and my chest can't stop caving
under the pressure of all this waiting
        for what?
        for when?
I don't know why I'm here
and I hate where I have been
I hope the darkness eats me whole
whatever is on the other side
        beats this hell of a home

Hell hole

Chapter 3 Creatures Of The Dark

Growing Gold

The night in me came out
                without warning
of the characters I'd find
                in the dark
I found it almost terrifying
                how quickly
I took on the part

The night in me

Growing Gold

When you blink, you know
>   your eyes are closed
but in pure pitch blackness
>   blinks become flinches
and your eyes don't know
>   if they are opened or closed
I've never been so blind
>   and I'm slowly losing my mind
because now the blackness is starting to
dance
>   and colours are swirling
yet I can't see my hands
where does it come from,
the dizziness I see
have I hit rock bottom?
>   is madness finally setting in on me?

Mad colours

Growing Gold

It felt like I was drowning
                in a dense fog of dreams
it was all so terrifyingly real
                and yet not what it seemed
the fog was a hot smoke
emitting from beneath me
and the dream was not so dreamlike
        because pain didn't escape me
I had caught my foot in a hidden crevice
        between time and reality
and in the far distance I could hear
        a freight train coming

Dead man waiting

Growing Gold

The dark side of the moon
        is a cold jealous witch
who envies high noon so much so
she turned her back on the world
        to plot her revenge
and the day she returns
        is the day
        all days will end

The dark side is calling

Growing Gold

Our suffering

is the same

yet we know

                nothing

of our shared pain

Pass the pain

I've learned to be
       very protective of
             my energy and space
because I know people
       and people love to take

Space

Growing Gold

My childhood home
      burned down

      after we moved

      because I wasn't there

      to guard

      the gates of hell

I had opened

         so it all came loose

Childhood doom

Growing Gold

Who we meet in the dark

        reflects

who we truly are

so if you can only find

        fake friends

with dirty minds

take a hard look at

        who you have become

We are one

Growing Gold

Everyone I meet
means something to me
whether it's a lesson learned
or a fond memory
and sometimes you need to meet people
that show you
it's time to change the locks
so no one can enter
with their old keys

Old keys

Growing Gold

Sleeping in while the sun blinds
                              the elderly
snoozing deeply
as the dawn scorches playgrounds
                              and cemeteries
yawning at the heat
like this hell feels refreshing
                              and mild to me

Accustomed to the heat

Growing Gold

You are but

        a footnote

on my journey

        a speck

        of a number

with a fine print meaning

that can only be found

        on the very last page

between other events

that aren't worth the energy

it takes to explain

just an afterthought

        a minor detail

one that carries no weight

        you are nothing

        but a sliver

in the spine of my story

I plucked you out

bled very little

        and healed instantly

Growing Gold

you are barely even
    a complete memory

Back story

Growing Gold

In my dreams
        I'm competing
and my rival wins
        deservedly
tears flood my face
        and I scream
waking up in this
        fine and feminine reality
as I open my eyes
        I unclench my fists
and grind my teeth
        all I want is to throw my hands
in your direction
        but I am civilized
so I plot your demise
        secretly

Fight dream

Growing Gold

Stuck in this ego
with its Stockholm ways
      I want to go home
but you tempt me to stay

Captured

Growing Gold

How many times
can we tell the same story—
one about chaos,

      horror,

            love and glory?

They told us before
but I'll have to say it again
how quickly our billions

            seem to forget

History all over again

Growing Gold

What colour do you bruise
　　　if not blue and green
how human are you
if you don't blink
　　　or dream
I've fallen and broken
　　　my shin or knee
but you won't make eye contact
because you're ashamed
　　　that I'm so weak

Broken and dirty

Growing Gold

The strangled cries of soft girls
      and the choking sighs of boys with
curls
shaking with fear from across the room
I can't see in this darkness
      but I can sense you
touching blindly, I feel your wounds
speaking softly,
        I comfort you
moving slowly,
        I introduce you two
there's no need for us to be so miserable
      in solitude

Three is company

Growing Gold

 My corporeal suit

doesn't fit like it used to

the ghost in me needs something new

  and if I shed my skin

  I'll be vulnerable again,

but living as a martyr in costume

is far from a virtue

  I know what I need to do

Shedding

Growing Gold

You've become a ghost

                              trapped in a game

that children play on Halloween

they knock on your doors

                              and scream in your

face

After an eternity of solitude

you thought opening up

would bring an act of grace,

                    proof of good

But instead you got

                    snot nosed youth

who take pleasure

in interrupting your melancholy

not realizing that this could very well

                    end up being their destiny

Ouija

Growing Gold

It feels so good

                being this evil

yet seeming so sweet

to the ignorant eyes

of unconfirmed enemies—

my friends

          until proven guilty

Not so pretty

Growing Gold

Why are you so full
    of memories
when you swore to banish
  the darkness
  from remembering
he didn't forget you
he might still be waiting
   the demon that breathes
   in between your heart beats
he watches while you're dreaming

Repressing

Growing Gold

How do I know what is
      and isn't
            supposed to be
when life sends me mixed signals
and dreams
that can't come true
how do I know who I am
            and who I should have been
            are we one and the same?
is there any point in asking?

Constant questioning

Growing Gold

I've fallen into a ditch
     and turned it into a grave
the crows are picking away
     at my miserable remains
take it all,
     my flesh
     my bones
this skeleton resembles
no one I know
I hear them pulling,
     tearing into my skin,
ripping apart the prison
     I'm caged within
and with every bite
their beaks take
a window reveals
     the wisdom
behind the seeming disorder
     of fate

Grave fate

Growing Gold

I shared a meal with the devil

and decided

he isn't so bad

we bonded over rejection,

      our fear of never being loved

and how we will never be able to compare

      to the man above

we laughed in the face of glory

and agreed

      that the light was for the fools

only the strong can be this heavy

and only the damned

      can truly understand

          how pain can be fuel

Dinner with the devil

Growing Gold

Face to face

with my ego

and every alternate state it takes

    from a ferocious vixen

    with eyes like a snake

to an innocent child

and their crude mistakes

Chest to chest

with my pride

    I see the cracks in my hide

        how my roar cuts deeper

        than my bite

Toe to toe

with my soul

and the universe it calls home

    I remember

    that I am not just one

        but one with all

Growing Gold

and despite this pain

I am not insane

    and certainly not

        alone

Ego to ego

Growing Gold

And so what if my friends
are just as broken as me
      and their teeth aren't aligned
      and their clothes are dirty
these exterior features,
      they show
         nothing
of the quality
    of their heartbeats
their flesh may not be pretty
but they are falling apart
while they hold me

Dead friends

Growing Gold

Fighting off the blues
gives me black eyes
and a big purple bruise
      under the skin
           behind my heart
where my spirit lives
     in hiding
     licking my wounds
as a last resort

Black and blue

Growing Gold

Your demons don't die
    they dissolve
and rematerialize

Demons don't die

Growing Gold

 Look both ways before
crossing deserted streets
because you never know when
someone might teleport
                while speeding

Irrational fears

Growing Gold

When my fish died
> I screamed

I hated the way it looked at me

just lying there,
> floating

wake up! start swimming!

I hate this,
> *you disgust me*

you lifeless glaring fish
> *you are worth nothing*

Dead pets, never again

Growing Gold

Hello madness,

     sadness

     and fragments of sanity

what have you done with the remains

     of my humanity?

Who told you about my hiding spots

the places I keep all my

     treasured hurt and

     tortured thoughts

they were never meant to be seen.

But now I see,

     you have seen everything

and there's no sense hiding

what has just been exposed.

Please bear with me

     because it's hard to stay composed

when all your secrets take form

     grow arms

Growing Gold

     and punch holes
in the walls
     built specifically to prevent me
from revealing my old bones.

Skeletons

Growing Gold

My dear slave sister,
I heard they stole you and took you
from your home
        bred you to make soldiers
hurt you so you could grow.

My sweet old mother
my broken aunts
        and daughters
I'm so sorry they ripped you
before you could reap
from the land you had sown.

But if it weren't for the madness,
and collective cruelty
        of our fathers
I wouldn't be here giving birth
        to the new world order.

Growing Gold

Your suffering is not without justice
        we are not destined to be martyrs
        we are sirens of tomorrow,
           we are the fire starters.

Stolen sisters

Growing Gold

Disowned
      and dishonoured
my bruises bring shame to my father
      my mother sobs
and my brother hides
      he knows there is a fury
brewing inside

Fight night

Growing Gold

I'm guilty of greed

    revenge

    and envy

I see now how my desires

    hurt more

    than just me

how could I be so blind

to the ripples of my fury

crossing off my foes

    forcing the hand of fate

    in the name of justice

        fear

        and hate

I see now

that I've dug myself this grave

and I'll be buried alive

    by my wrath

    and myopic gaze

So nearsighted it's blinding

Growing Gold

I hurt you

because you deserved it

and in doing so

asked for the hurt

      back

and forth

      we exchange pain

down every path

like hot potato

      making even

on the crimes of our past

but never letting go

Justice in the wrong hands

Growing Gold

What leaves my mouth

                becomes your sounds

and so we take turns

spitting up our nightmares

                and deepest fears

without realizing our similarities

                are so severe

we practically share

            the same eyes

            and ears

We share here

Growing Gold

If there is only one second
        worth regretting
it's the one I didn't seize
the one
        where I hesitated
the one where
        I chose to hold on
        instead of being free
so now I will wait
for fate
to release me

Release

Growing Gold

My mirror never lies
it shows me the truth
     naked and dirtied
     with poor light
because I never open the windows
and refuse to look deeper
than the skin I'm dressed in
blue veins web
     over my chest and
     reveals the fiend
that lies within
the creature of my flesh
     the reality of my sins

Beneath the skin

Growing Gold

I chose to fight myself
        instead of my demons
because I really couldn't blame them
        when I was the one
who invited them over to begin with
        I egged them on
said I doubted their strength
so they brought all their friends
        and told me to say it to their face
what an idiot I was
for starting wars I had no right to finish
        so I chose to self-destruct
to be completely assured
        we would mutually combust
and still,
        it felt like winning

Mutually assured destruction

Growing Gold

There's a world inside
that must be braved
      an inner cavern
      a hermit's cave
where you can spend your mornings
      in silence before the sun
then crawl down deeper
until you're one
         with all the monsters
      from which
      you wish to run
hold their hand
and send them love
instead of the hate that birthed them
         in the first place

Born from hate

Growing Gold

I can take a punch

                 and fight

with every cell I divide

I can duck a blow

        throw a hook

        knock out a tooth

                and still lose

but even in defeat

I'll know in my soul

I gave it my all

        even when I had so little

I kept the fire alive

        while nights grew cold

and even when my teeth chattered

and the crowds booed

                I kept up the hype

                and roared with the night

        I do what I do

to keep it a fair fight

Fair fight

Growing Gold

The truth will set you free
      but first
might punish you severely
for the length of time
you keep it hidden
         is paid in threes
to heal you from the darkness
and secret disease
the sooner you bring it to
         the light
the sweeter the remedy

Sweet truth

Growing Gold

So you want to tell stories
about how you tore me
apart
      from my orifices
forcing me into a state of
non-consensual metamorphoses
I wish I could've called it
but had I been able to foresee
I would've killed the opportunity
and wouldn't have grown
out of spite
        so exponentially

Growing despite

Growing Gold

I had a dream

    I was potting a plant

with green and purple leaves

when I heard a deep man's voice

speak within me

    water it

I felt the reverberation

and came to the realization,

he wasn't just talking about the plant

    I need to water me

Water dreams

Growing Gold

Even though I'm afraid of
the glowing exit sign
      I can still show you the way
the light is blinding
but I know I'll pass through
      it one day
and until my time arrives
let me be your guide
I've been in the dark for so long
my eyes need to adjust
      I might be here a while

Left in the dark

Growing Gold

I can't let my love
                  deflate
and I can't watch my hero
                      shrug off his fate
so I'll drop my darkness
           and turn on my light
hoping to guide your way
while my dirty laundry
           continues to pile

Your light

Chapter 4 Becoming Light

Growing Gold

    Am I
a flimsy ego
or a spirit made
of gold
    am I
just a soul
or can I also have
physical goals

Am I gold?

Growing Gold

Don't sit there looking dumb

with sadness dripping

      from your lashes

you'll only drown yourself in puddles

or worse,

      sicken with madness

take my hand

let me elevate you

      just a little

I can help you climb out of this

temporary darkness

find your footing

      bring you to my level

it's not that much better,

but at least now you're not alone

and now we can search for the light

      together

Lighter

Growing Gold

Once I realized that
my daydreams became realities
I began to dream of grand
and miraculous fantasies

If my horrors can come through

then so too can my wildest

and ambitious reveries

they all come true

Daydreams

Growing Gold

I've seen some major forks in my day
and every time I turn away
      from the path of my mother,
      my ancestors,
I am greeted with a fate
that was so obviously designed
      just for me
that I can't help but think
          these decisions
      are the threads
that make up the fabric
      that is destiny

Destined to be me

Growing Gold

I believe in the power
    of the mighty beyond
                  so
I grew roots that vibrate religiously
    but the reality of truth
    hangs like a web
             invisibly
and can only be known by instinct
with flashes of sudden tickles
and lots of shivering

Shivering instinct

Growing Gold

One man's tool
is another man's torture

What works for you
       may not work for another
so keep your trash
       but share your treasure

One man's peace
is another man's pressure

Treasured pressure

Growing Gold

It's not a darkness
                    that suddenly hits
but a gradual overcast
            and subtle gloom
that loves to rain
                    on top of you
I felt it before
                    I've been in the mist
of a never ending
ocean storm
I was tossed and tormented
until my screams drowned
                        in the wind
I fought for so long
even when all I wanted
                        was to give in
I couldn't catch a breath
or a moment of rest
and just staying afloat
                        was tedious at best
But despite the temptation

Growing Gold

to let go

to give in

I kept fighting the storm

while I dreamed of

clear skies

and sun beams on my skin

I can't remember how long

I spent wrestling

with the shadows of tidal waves

the darkness felt infinite

and I was suffocating

the moment was forever

and a part of me is still there

but now I no longer spar

with hurricanes

or tsunamis

now I sail high and ride

the waves that used to hunt me

because there came a time

when I stopped being sad,

tired,

Growing Gold

         defeated,

                and unfeeling

and instead I became

        enraged,

            rabid,

                and fuming

I took my anger out

on the light house that never

                helped

and the ships that were too big

to see me drowning

           by myself

I can't remember how

but I found myself ashore

after countless nights

           of salt stung eyes

and relentless tossing

             between tides of torture

the static land confused my body

my knees didn't know which way to bend

before I could walk,

Growing Gold

                    I was forced to crawl again
from all fours I stood myself up
and slowly began to march my way
to the lighthouse above
                    furious that its light
                    refused to guide me home
angry at all the time I wasted
          lost in the cyclone
          suffering for no one
                    sinking like a stone
I climbed the spiralled stairs
          resisting the nightmare
broke down the door and found
a burnt-out beacon
          and despite not having my own light
          or knowledge of electrical currents
I set out to reignite
the pathfinding lantern
I took the fire that burned through my heart
          the ire that threatened to boil over
          poured it into the spotlight beaker

Growing Gold

I emptied my chest
from all the fury I had caged
and soon enough
the light house began

                        to re-illuminate

in ways I had never seen light behave

                        a white hot glow

flash flooded the small room
and spilled out into the night
where the darkness loomed
I directed the beacon
towards the tormenting ocean

        hoping to guide home

anyone else who might feel broken

Light beacon

Growing Gold

I am the gold
       that Midas stole
and used to kill his family
I am a weapon
       sharp and shining
a curse dressed up
       like a luxurious blessing

Careful what you wish for
       because I can bring you greed
careful how you love me
       because if it's not real,
              I'll turn you green.

Gold touch

Growing Gold

I ignored the voices in my head
after being told
   they couldn't be trusted
that they weren't my voices
and they came from
   unsavoury sources
but as always
     I refused to listen
to those who dictate my limitations
I introduced myself
   to my voices
and found out they belonged
   to my inner children
     of past generations
they whisper songs
    of intuition
tell me when to run or stay
tell me stories
    through imagination
and dreams of the day
now I trust my inner child

Growing Gold

teach her to be careful
               and brave
and in return she keeps me wild
in the creative and playful
               kind of way

Inner voices

Growing Gold

Be the honey

        not the bee

slather your love

in smooth,

      sticky,

        memories

that sweetens bitter teas

 be the nectar

        collected busily

stored until winter

to spread some sunny

Be the juice of flowers

      preserved

      and perfuming

fields upon fields

      of sun salutations

be the imperishable remedy

you yourself need

Be honey

Growing Gold

Still stagnant pools
and old dirty shoes
    you're rotting away
and growing mildew
as a part of you dies
    newness is born
it might make you sick
        at first
but in time
a new gold will be born

New gold

Growing Gold

Different seeds
        different flowers
we carry the codes
        to fertilize our power

Flower power

Growing Gold

So slow

and infinitely tedious

                progress

      means pain

victory

      takes strain

gold can't be formed

         willy nilly

it takes exact measurements

      of pressure

      and heat

to turn iron into something

that glows brilliantly

without also feeding

      your secret greed

you won't find the treasure

      until you're treasure worthy

Treasure hungry

Growing Gold

My heart aches for resolve
      for you to find your fire
but I know it may take a while
and I can wait
I have faith in all things destiny
      and I love you
            like I love fate

Soul mates

Growing Gold

The sun slipped

between the cracks in the clouds

and told me

I shouldn't be afraid

to be loud

Good morning

Growing Gold

Healing starts
      at the hardest part
      when you're too broken to feel
      so collect your dust
      and fragments of trust
      your wounds have magic to reveal.

Magic pain

Growing Gold

We get sick
      and we heal
      we fall
but then soon rise
      no gravity
      nor virus
can keep us
from marching on
and slowly
      growing wise.

Uphill wisdom

Growing Gold

What used to feel like
　　　being a hamster
racing furiously on a wheel
now feels like
　　　a dog chasing
a rabbit
　　　nipping at its heel

Getting closer

Growing Gold

Humble yourself
with gratitude
because that's all pain
will teach you

Painful gratitude

Growing Gold

Everything is passing,
      but you are not the breeze
you are not passing
you are a turbine
      built to harness energy

Everything is passing

Growing Gold

Sometimes I get so high
off the words of the wise
    I dare let myself feel like god
but I would never dare
worship my own power
    because a true god creates
with or without prayer

We are god

Growing Gold

Light a fire,
       literally
light a candle and watch it glow
soak yourself in the presence
of its ever-changing flow
learn what it means to inspire
       to spark and excite,
understand what it means to become
and then destroy everything in sight
       light yourself on fire
and watch your heart glow bright

Light yourself on fire

Growing Gold

I am the eye

of the storm that bellows

surrounded by

      daunting pressure

yet unmoved and unbothered

because destruction is just

      another treasure

Storming

Growing Gold

Destroy everything,
>>smiling
because chaos is another kind
>>of creativity
and here we are
soaking in
the smithereens
>>of artistry

Destroy everything

Growing Gold

I need you to hold me down

because I feel like I'm about to crack open

and release a million

        butterflies

I need you to ground me

        be my tree

I need to get rooted

because right now

        I'm high flying

Need grounding

Growing Gold

I told my mother

    not to worry

but hearing the words

made me feel better

like I needed to hear it

    say it out loud

that I will be okay

    that this is temporary

that I have the strength

to find my way out

of the deep end

    this dead end

everything will be just fine

I just need to take my time

    but thank you for asking mom

I needed to hear it for myself

Telling you, telling me

Growing Gold

Look up—
          there is an entire endless
spinning chandelier
          now look down—
at those puddles too shallow
for you to drown
do you see the reflection?
the ant sized twinkling
don't you see
that the above
is the below
          reflecting

As above

Growing Gold

Love doesn't last
        but neither does misery
the best we can hope for
are a few moments
        of stability

It's all temporary

Growing Gold

If I'm hungry for blood
>then I will let myself bleed
because no hunger of mine
>can ever be pleased
unless it comes directly
>from me

Blood thirsty

Growing Gold

Sometimes the worst
happens for good reason
      it's just a shame we can't
      peak behind the curtain
and see the magic
      that puts on the show
the backstage trickery
      that suspends everything
      you think you know

The worst happens

Growing Gold

I am seeing the change

I want to be

the world is out there

     and in here,

          it's all me

if I breakdown,

     no one can save me

you can hold my hand

     but can't change anything

experience is the only

teacher I need

Experience learning

Growing Gold

On the contrary,

    I survived

your attempts at

stripping my spirit

only slightly scratched my mind

my body took a couple hits

my heart,

   endured and bloody

I toed the threshold

    of life and death

I revolted against my body

given the torment

and invasion of my psyche

no one expected

   I'd make it out alive

they thought I'd give in to decline

but oh—quite the contrary

   I stood up,

     and I survived

On the contrary

Growing Gold

Seeds breed inside
 the muscle tissue
  of my mind
germinating furiously
spreading wildfire
  illuminating the divine
I plant not only fruit
 but hardy wholesome weeds
because the hills call for more
than mangos and melodies
I need fertile thoughts
 unbounded creativity
that answers the call of the wind
to live life blazing
  curiously

Windy

Growing Gold

In and out
of my body experience
      letting go
of my flesh bound home
there's a world within
      and a world without
and I am Joan of arc
to my fate,
      I am devout

Joan of fate

Growing Gold

Fire sparks from friction
        constant grinding
        repetitive actions

Smoking up frayed hairs
        constant grinding
        repetitive actions

Disintegrating what is left
        constant grinding
        repetitive actions

And just when you think
all you can make are plumes
        lightning strikes
        in a single molecule

Combustion and energy
moving too quickly
until it's impossible to contain
        growing exponentially

The dead wood
      that was left to rot
has become a reckoning force
      born to be born
from constant grinding
and repetitive actions

Born to be

Growing Gold

Growth looks so
> damn easy

but it hurts more that it seems

the pain is excruciating

bones stretch lengthening
> popping

ripping my skin at the seams

leaving scars and stripes

but I'm feeling less like tigers
> and more like mice

Mouse life

Growing Gold

I feel like puking up
all this poisoned blood
that's been sitting stagnant
    at the bottom of my belly
and now that I'm boiling
my ego from the inside
I feel the urge
    to purge
    my impurities.

Purging

Growing Gold

Even breaking isn't so bad
just look at what happened
when the moon
       collided with the land
she gave us new dust
       and spores
that fell to the bottom
       of our ocean floors
giving something new
for the sun to feed
something to create a new you,
       a new me

New moon

Growing Gold

I have a solar powered soul
that feels like sugar in my body

    light desires light

and I feel like blinding
     the creatures of the night
     the shadows of my ego
my spirit yawns,
       awakening
as the dawn unfolds

Dawning

Growing Gold

Pain is the perfect kindling

with its dry

     and dusty substance

catching spark

     and setting ablaze

to all that's dead

     and decomposing

Burning pain

Growing Gold

Everything is light
even your heaviest burdens
      have a flicker of the heavenly
there are no cold nights
      only warmer mornings
everything is light
      everything is moving

Everything is everything

Growing Gold

Burn hotter than your ego
       when it sees something
       it wants
let all your desires
       turn to dust
sweep up the ashes
and throw them into an iron pot

Fill your heart and soul with water
       and let the pot boil over
until all the moisture is gone
       when the steam dries out
refill and distill once more
       and again
refining your dreams
until all that remains
       is the glittering essence
              of how your childhood began

Now sprinkle that silver
       onto your garden bed

Growing Gold

be sure to mix with manure

because all that is meant to grow

        must be fed

        by death

and again your ashes will sprout

but before growing upwards

        they will grow low

spreading roots into the earth

taking hold before

        letting go

Once they break the surface

        and taste the light of gold

you'll be left with more bounty

than you thought you could ever sew

        with just your desires

        and your ego.

Growing gold

Growing Gold

And there we sat
                 perfectly aligned
on the axis of the Pacific
                   sunset
watching the neon fire
      sink
       into its reflection
I absorbed all its wisdom
as I balanced on the beams
                 between darkness
and perfection
and the dreamscape in between

The axis of reflection

Growing Gold

My spots are returning

metamorphosis

                and yearning

sprouts about doubts

tides can't stop turning

I love beginnings

       but my god

       how they hurt

growing pains like a teenager,

are there stretch marks

       on my heart?

Stretched heart

Growing Gold

You are not falling behind
as you watch the world pass by
     with an observant eye
I know you want to lead the race
but in the bigger picture
     the best
doesn't always mean
     first place

Best place

Growing Gold

Welcome to my inner monologue,
where my mother and father
      still don't get along
and their tension have become
      a kind of theme song
I am strong minded
      like my father,
with the stubborn will of my mom
put us all together and
we clash like floral and polka dots

Because of the economy
and our domestic
         cultural dichotomy
I was fertilized prematurely—
I grew up too soon,

I used to carry my father's worries,
and now
      "my mother once told me"
has become a frequent intro to a story.

Growing Gold

And if I become her, that's ok,
I just don't want to make
              the same mistakes
between her voice urging me
                      to always be free
and my father's lectures
        on excellency
I'm bound to do
        one
        of two things
I can either combust and implode
or I can make the most
        of this genetic mold
and since I am a hybrid
        of two different colours
I might as well celebrate being
              the incarnation of purple.

Purple

Growing Gold

Nature knows

not to force the flow

that's why leaves change

                  patiently

falling only when

they're ready to let go

Nature knows

Growing Gold

Change is beautiful
but is often caused by death
       a part of us
falls apart
so we can save what is good
and make room for progress

A good death

Growing Gold

Past the point
of no return
      is a plane of pure destiny
lying in the hands
      that opened the door
and ignored all the boundaries

Pushing boundaries

Growing Gold

I don't cast spells
                    I cause inspiration
these tricks you call magic
are just supreme wisdom

I lit a fire in your heart
and watched you float
                    into the heavens
what you call manifestation
                    I call pure vision

Magic is wisdom

Growing Gold

I surrender to my story
                I give in to fate
there's no way else
to find my way out
so I'll have to sit
                and wait

Hear my story

Growing Gold

What is it about willow trees
that feels so comforting
      they hang low
      rooted deep
soaking in the sweet ravine
I could sit beneath them
and listen to the wisdom
      of soft swaying leaves
there's something familiar
      about the way she breathes
like we have more in common
            than it seems
      she brings me peace
         I bring her stories
      reading from my memories
I can almost see her smiling
like she's been there
      like she was once a part of me
and as long as I give myself
to her grace and wonder
      I can subtly remember

Growing Gold

my days as a willow
and nights of star slumber

Basking in the willow

Growing Gold

I understand now how

    healing me

        cost you

an expensive amount of energy

and now you're sick

        sad

        and twisted

        into knots

you lay there wasted

as I stand up

but this rebirth was not for nothing

if there's one thing I have learned

it's how to give

        and take love

and I have taken so much from you

I know now what I have to do

        I'll hold and heal you

        give you my patient heart

            spare some fire

            keep you warm

Growing Gold

until you are reborn from the ashes
I won't fly until you can soar

Teaching you to fly

Growing Gold

Over a thousand missing pieces
        filled in with the molten
                gold of experience
      if I couldn't see the light
              between the cracks in our
      walls
how could I have known
              it was safe to fall
      and trust that this glue
              would hold us together
despite the risk of shatter
              I always cure my own
      disaster

Complete gold

Growing Gold

If I could go back in time
I wouldn't change
        a single thing
 where I am
was worth all the pain

In time

Growing Gold

Could this day be

any more beautiful

      any more bountiful

            any more abundant

and beaming with potential?

A good morning

Growing Gold

Unbound by time

free from segmented

divides

    present

and eternally resting

  with a smile

Zenning

Growing Gold

Every time I reach the end
of a chapter, a book,
      a ride,
or jump off the deep end
        and dive
I stay in awe
that I survived
enamoured by the fall
          so much so
that the end makes me cry
      again! again!
          one more time

One more time

Growing Gold

The golden hour glides
its blade
     through time
capturing the moment
        momentarily
a temporal halt
between the dark
     and light
it smells like the cusp
of awakening

On the cusp

Growing Gold

Everything in this life
is meant to be turned to gold
       your hate to love
           the hot to cold
every time you suffer
you come closer
         to pleasure
as long as you keep your heart open
to the pain
       and not disassociate
the world will transform around you
as you heal your burns
           and bones
you'll see your blood bleed brighter
as you become yourself, whole

Everything is gold

Growing Gold

I am

becoming

      expressing my word

          creatively

while spirit speaks to

      and through me

I am

living

      poetically

Becoming something

49465862R00131

Made in the USA
Columbia, SC
21 January 2019